BONES IN THE HUMAN BODY!
Anatomy Book for Kids

BABY PROFESSOR
EDUCATION KIDS

Speedy Publishing LLC
40 E. Main St. #1156
Newark, DE 19711
www.speedypublishing.com

Copyright 2016

All Rights reserved. No part of this book may be reproduced or used in any way or form or by any means whether electronic or mechanical, this means that you cannot record or photocopy any material ideas or tips that are provided in this book

Every human body has bones. Together they are called the skeleton. Your body has more than 200 bones. Each bone has a purpose.

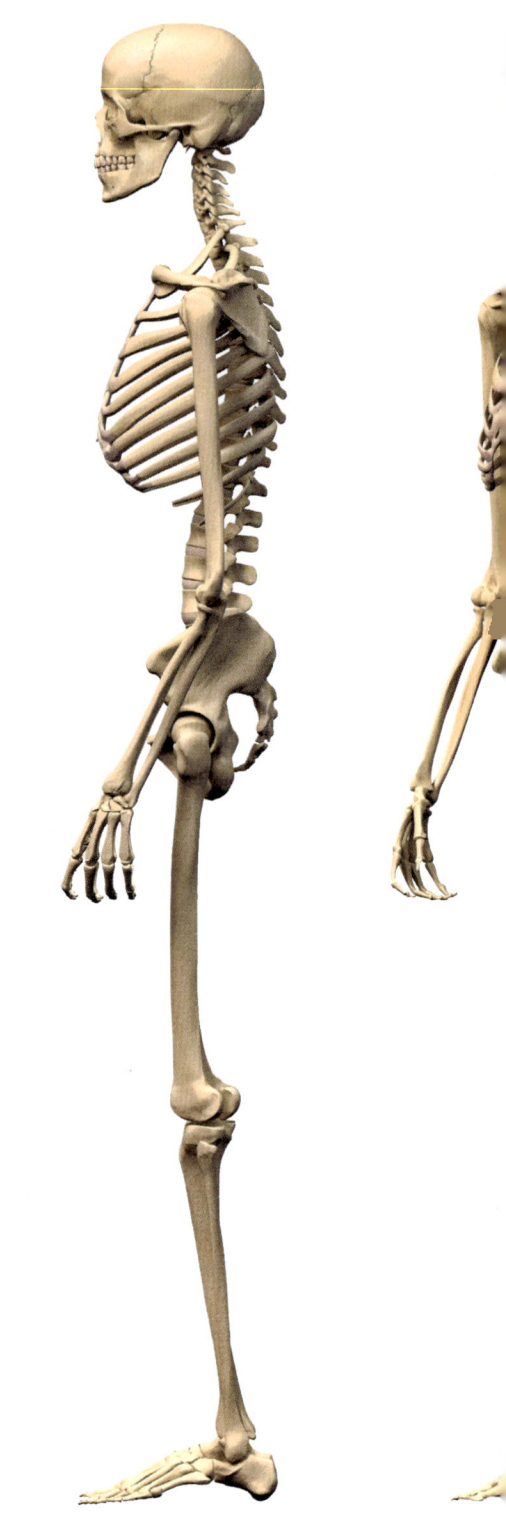

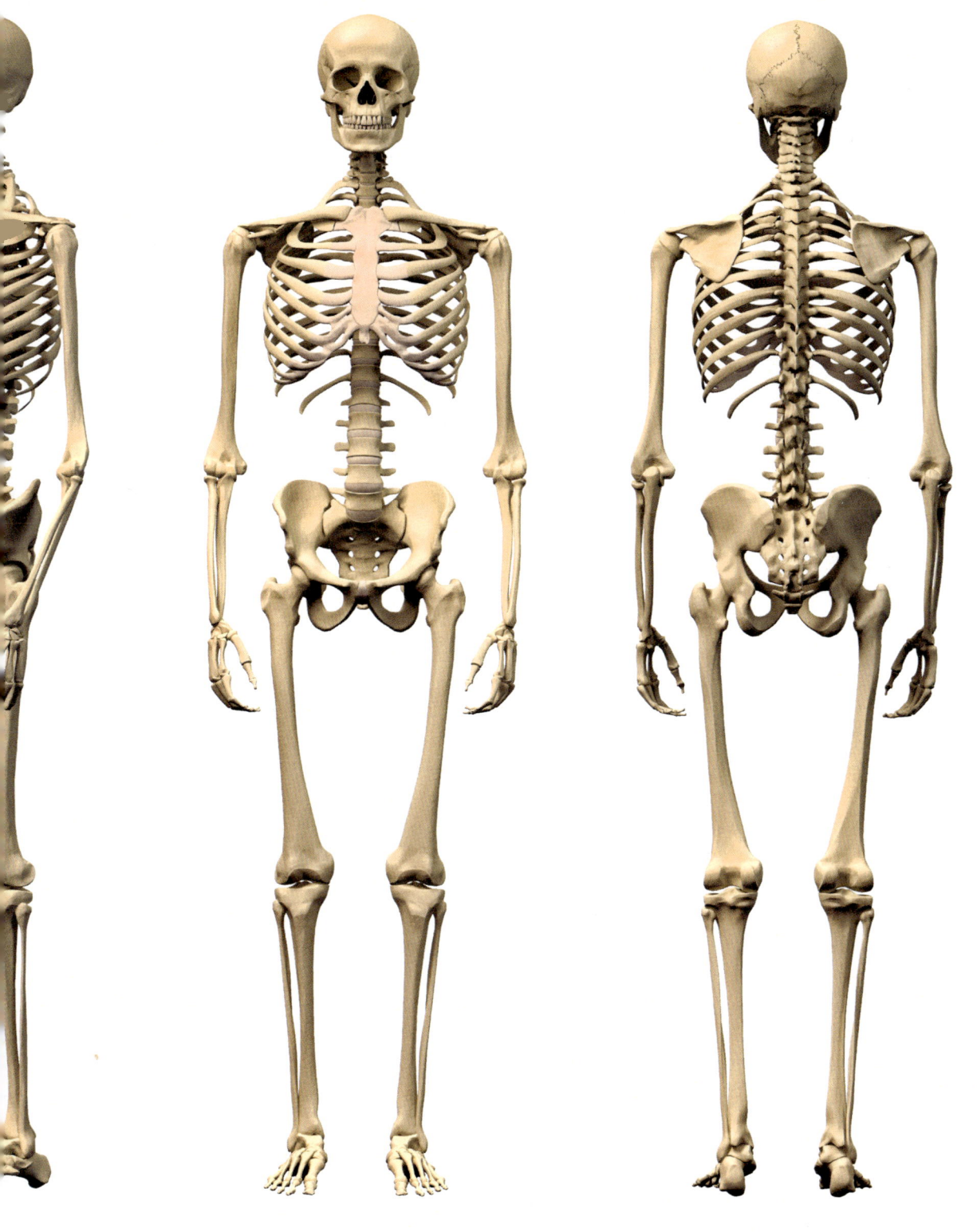

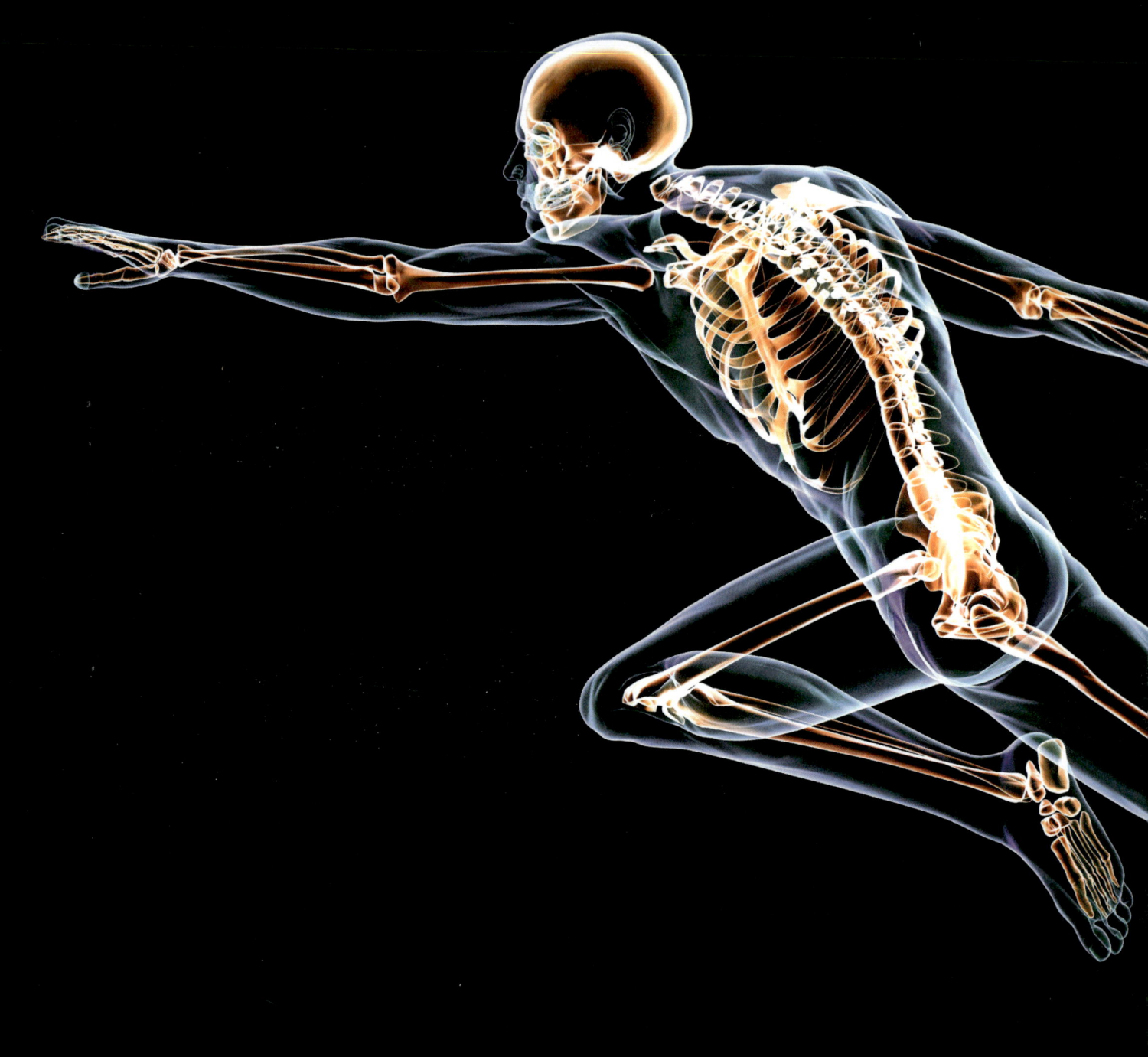

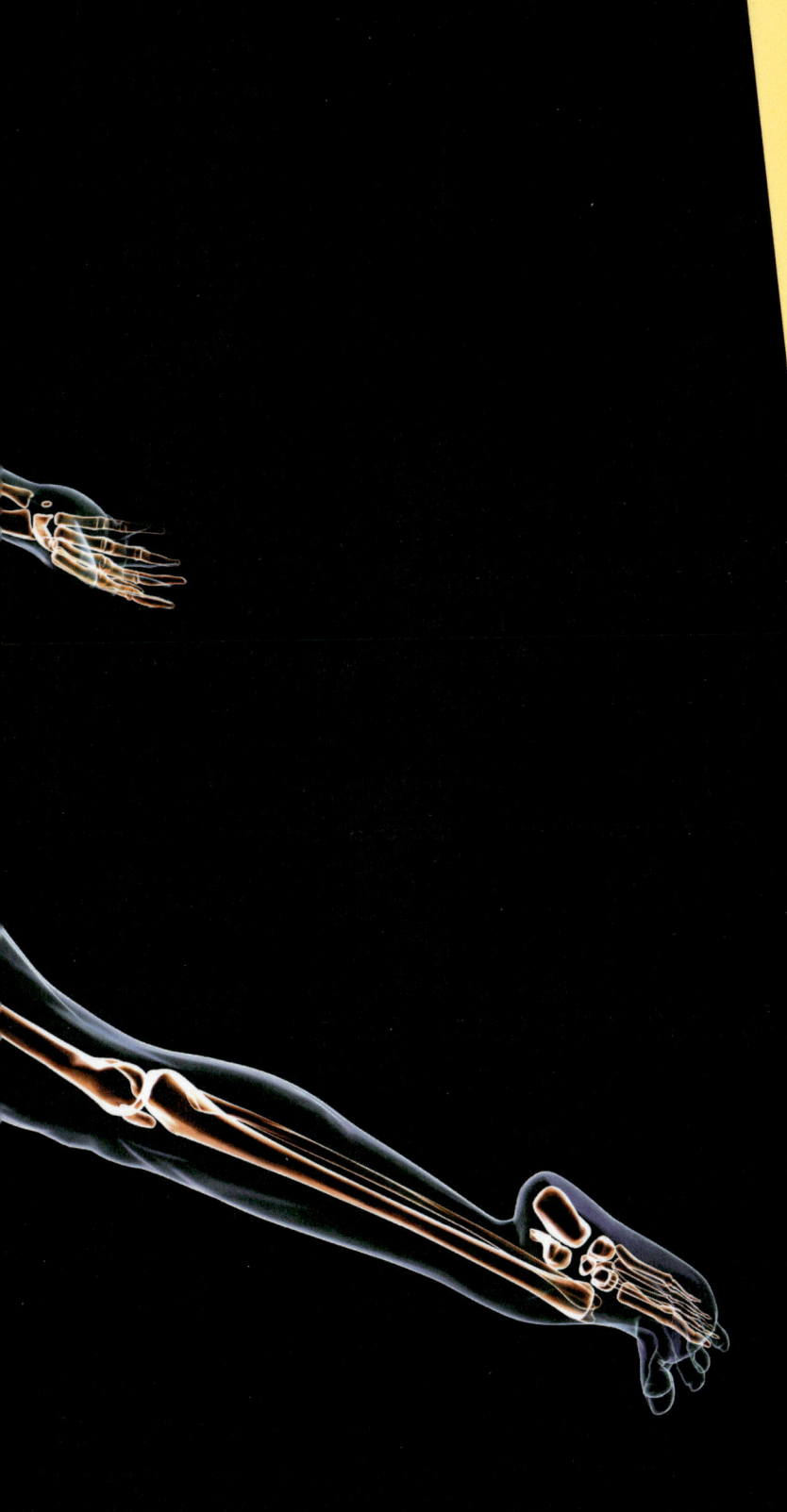

Our bones give our bodies shape. Their role is to support and protect our organs and systems. Our bones are very tough, so our skeleton can support our entire weight.

A skeleton looks kind of scary, but without it, everyone would look like a jellyfish. Our body parts are soft and squishy and the bones are hard and strong. Bones hold you up so you can move around.

The bones that make up your skeleton are living, growing and changing parts. Like other parts of your body, they grow big and strong over time.

Babies have more than 300 bones in their bodies, but as they grow up some bones merge together. As adults, they have about 200. Bones continue to grow from birth until our mid 20's. Our skeleton's bone mass is at its maximum thickness around the age of 30.

About 70% of your bones are made of hard minerals and calcium. Calcium is very important for your bones. It helps keep them strong and healthy.

Most bones have four parts, and almost every bone in your body is made of the same materials. The four parts are periosteum, compact bone, spongy bone, and bone marrow.

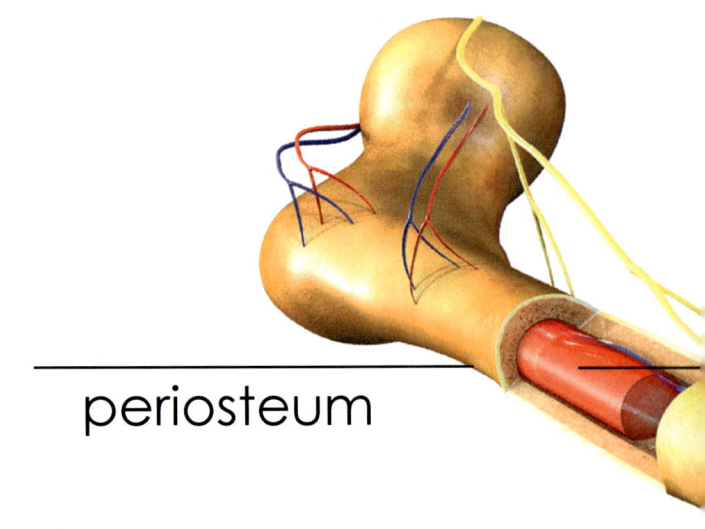

periosteum

compact bone

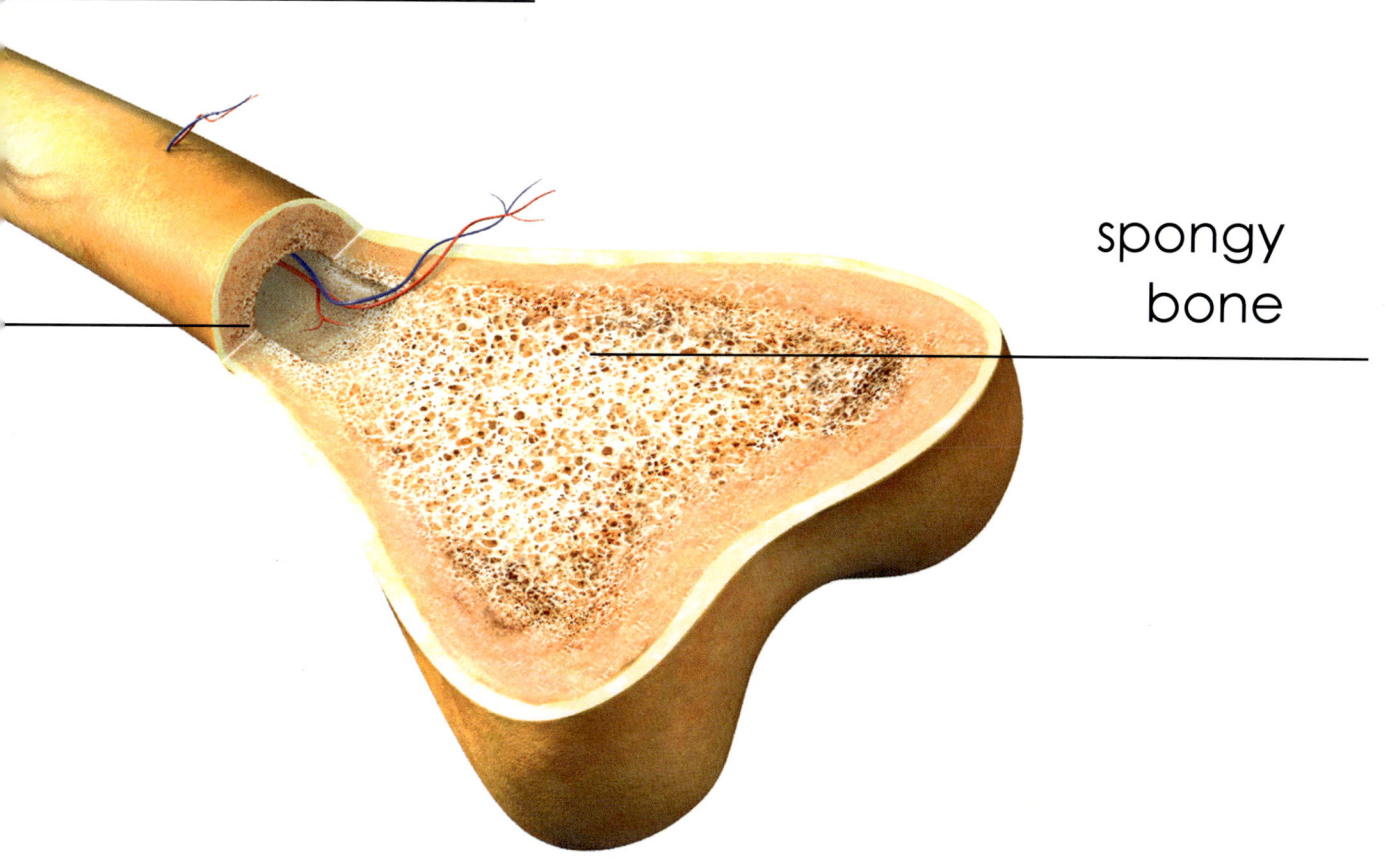

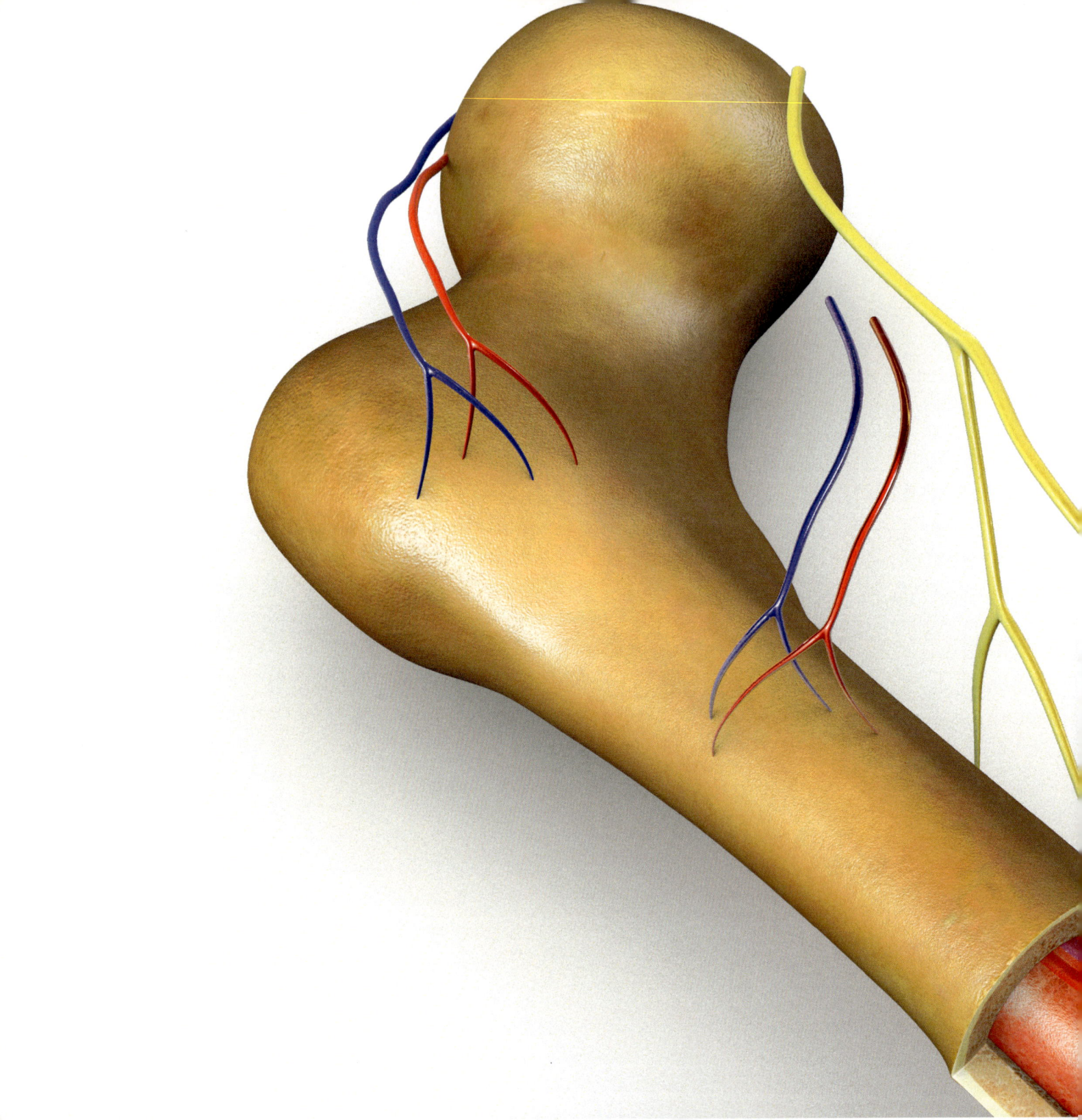

The outside part of a bone is the periosteum (per-ee-oss-tee-um). It's a thin, dense membrane that holds nerves and blood vessels that nurture the bone.

The next layer is made up of compact bone. This part is very smooth and hard. This is what we see when we look at a skeleton.

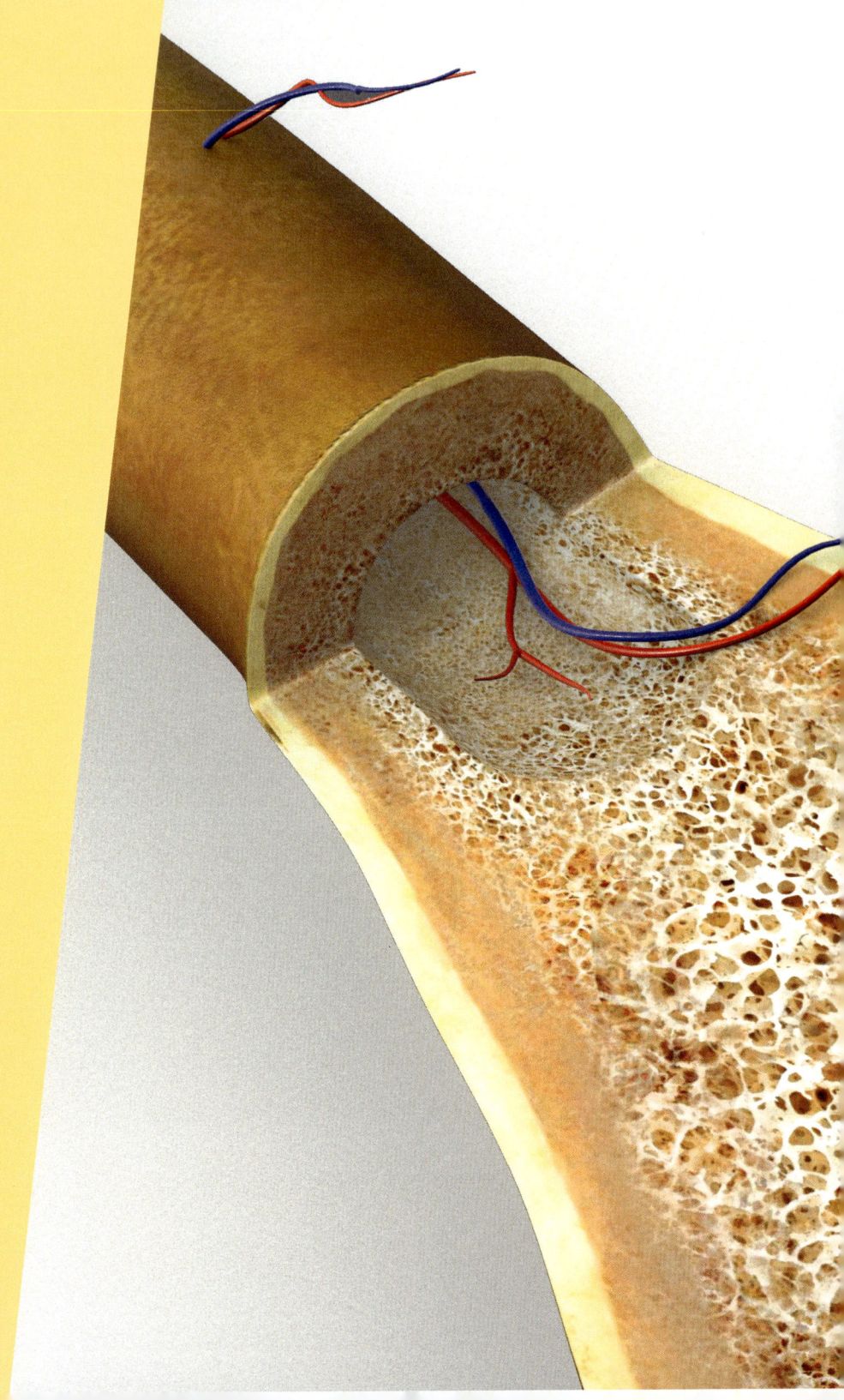

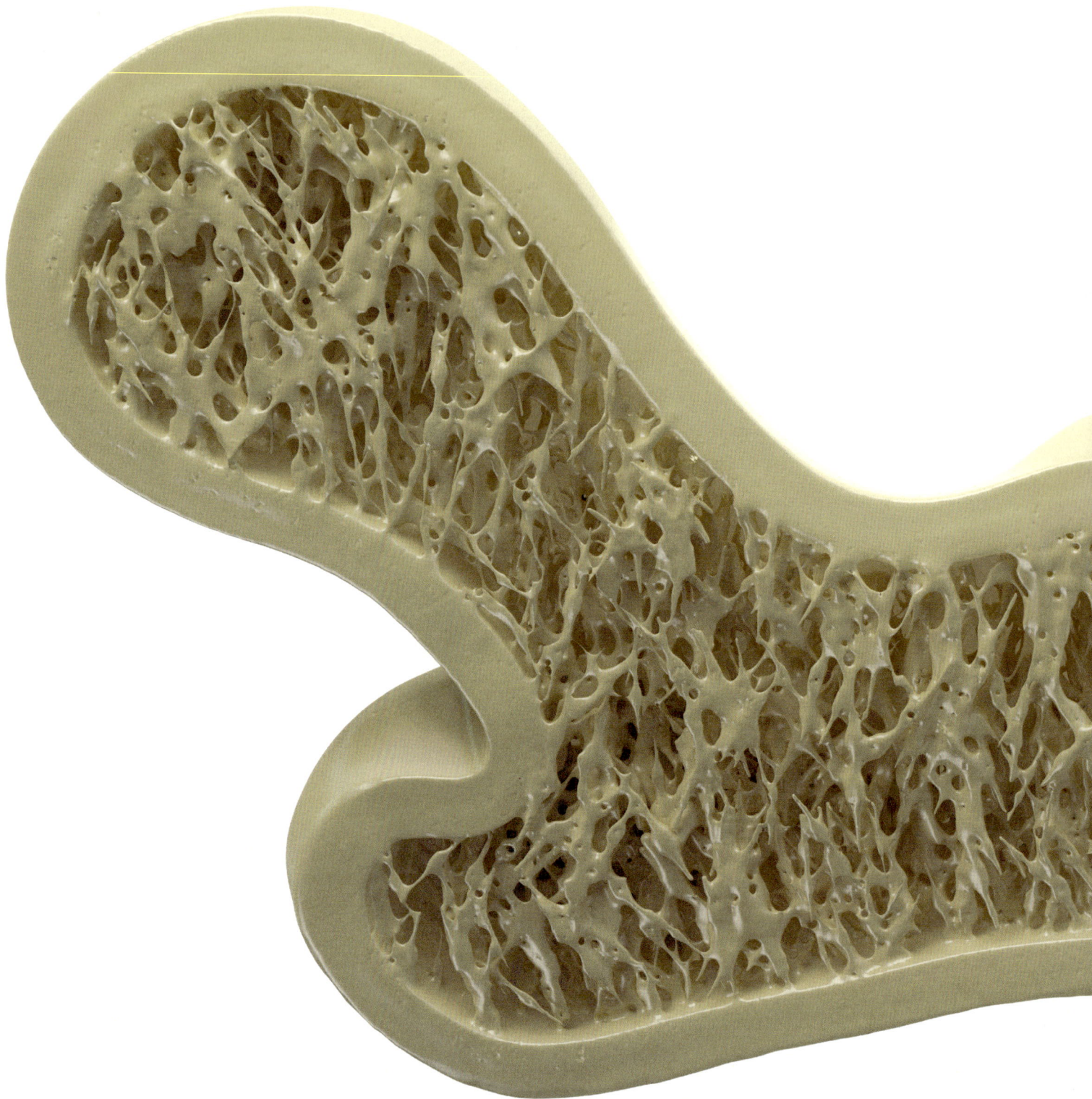

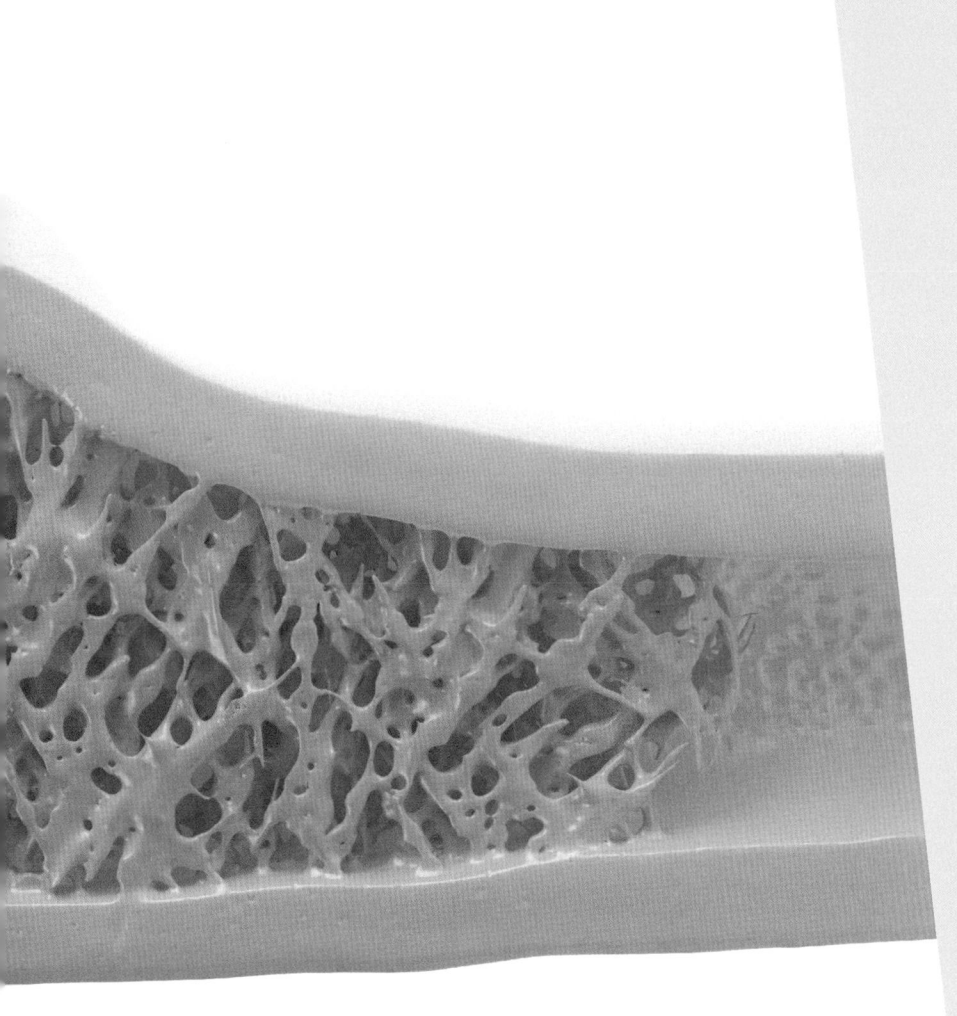

Spongy, or cancellous (can-sel-us) bone looks a bit like a sponge and protects the inner part of the bone. Cancellous bone is not as hard as compact bone, but it is still very strong.

The innermost part of the bone is the bone marrow. It looks a little like jelly, soft and flexible. It is very important because it helps make blood cells for your body.

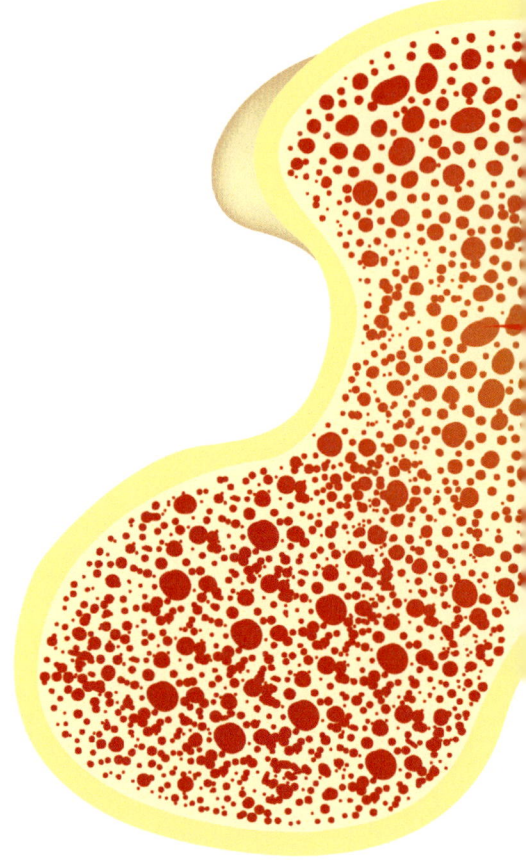

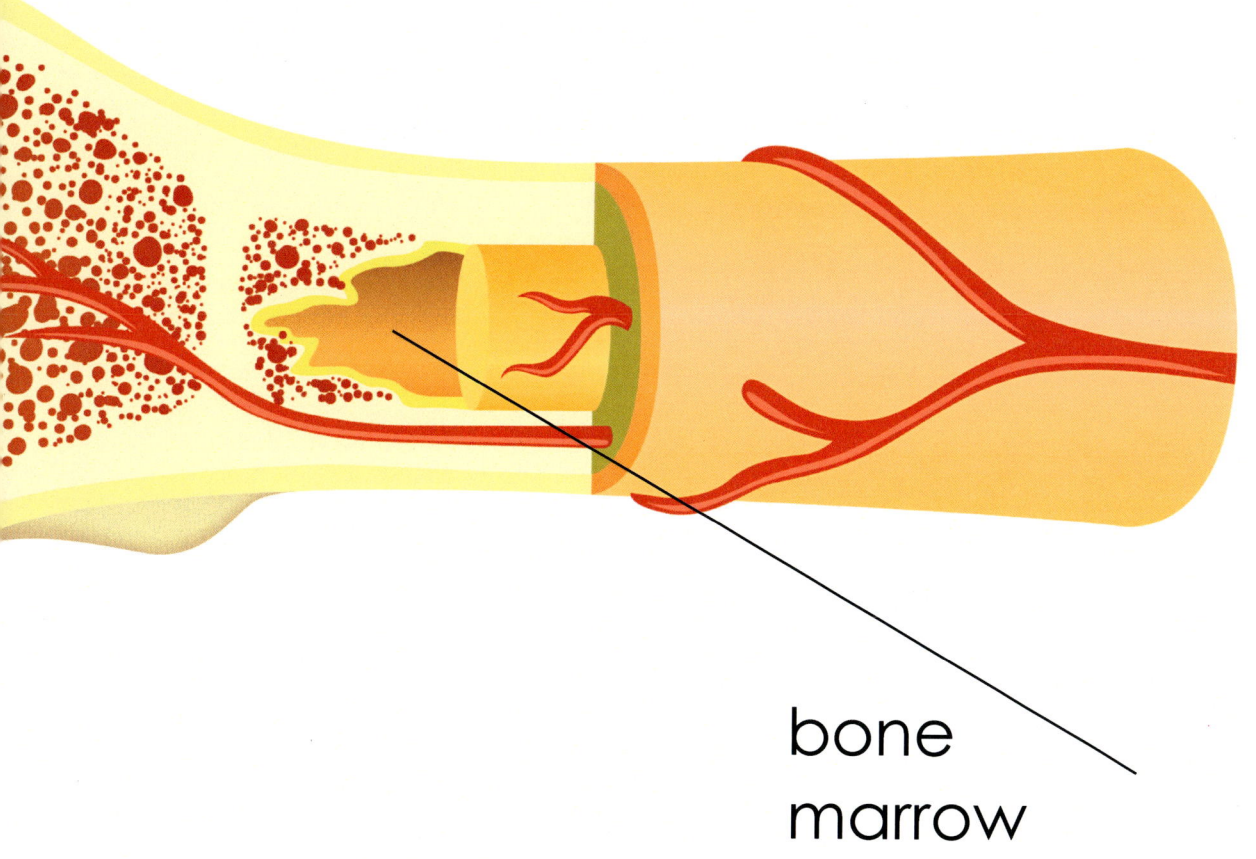

bone marrow

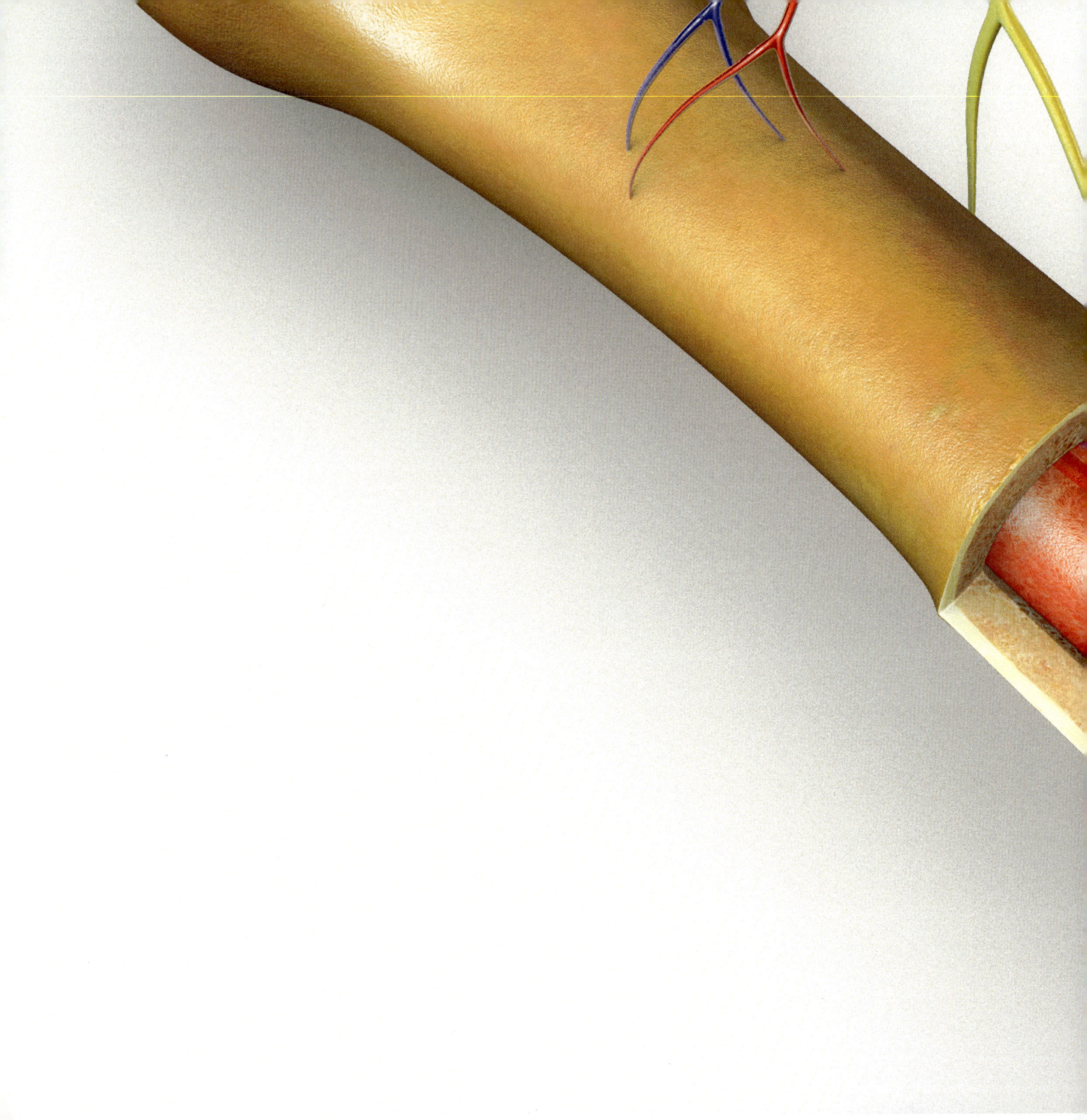

Your bone marrow makes up 4% of the human body mass. It also produces lymphocytes, which support our immune system.

Bones are connected to each other by joints. Because of the joints the bones can move and our body can bend. Joints also work to lessen friction and pillow the bones against impact.

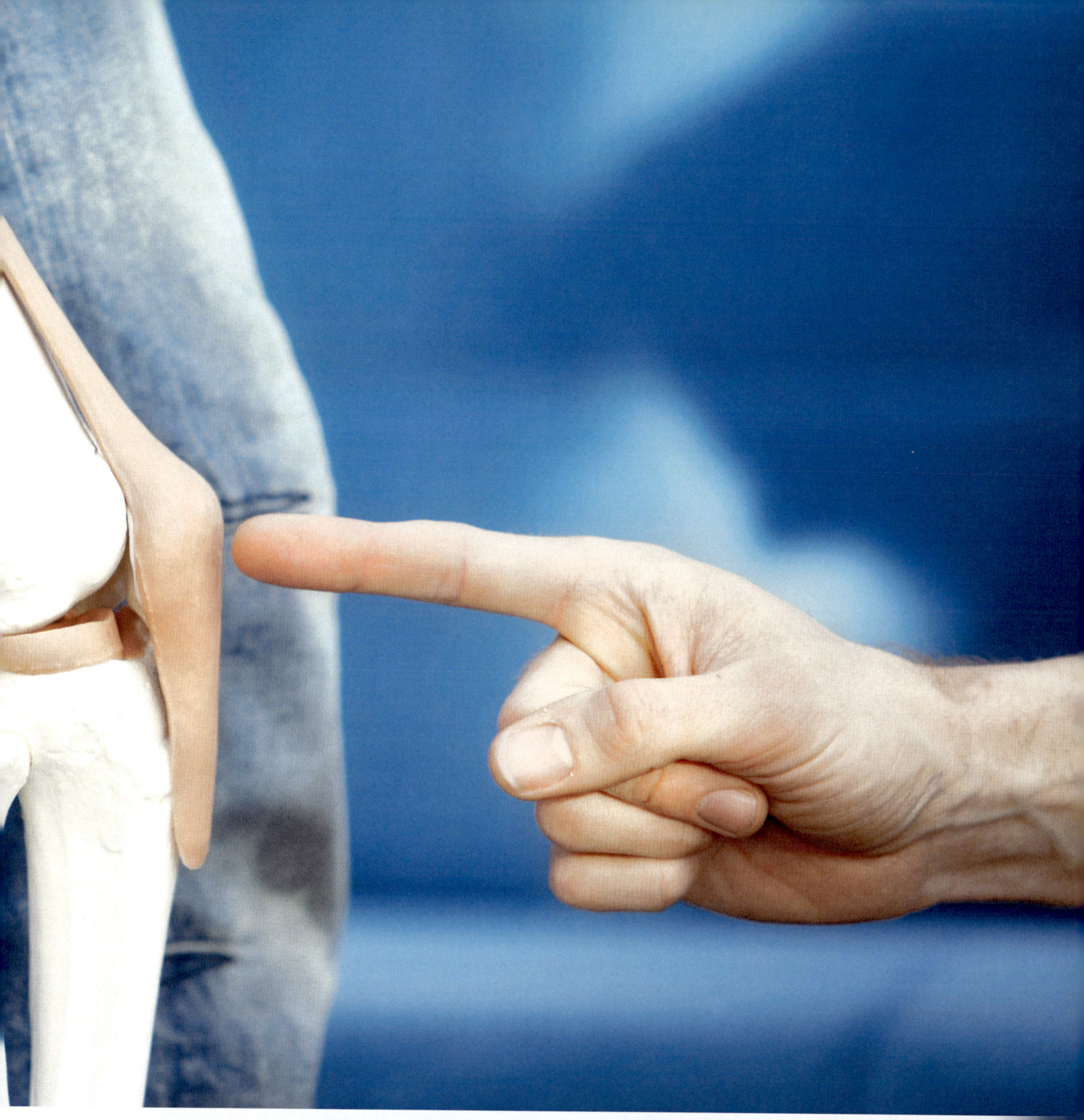

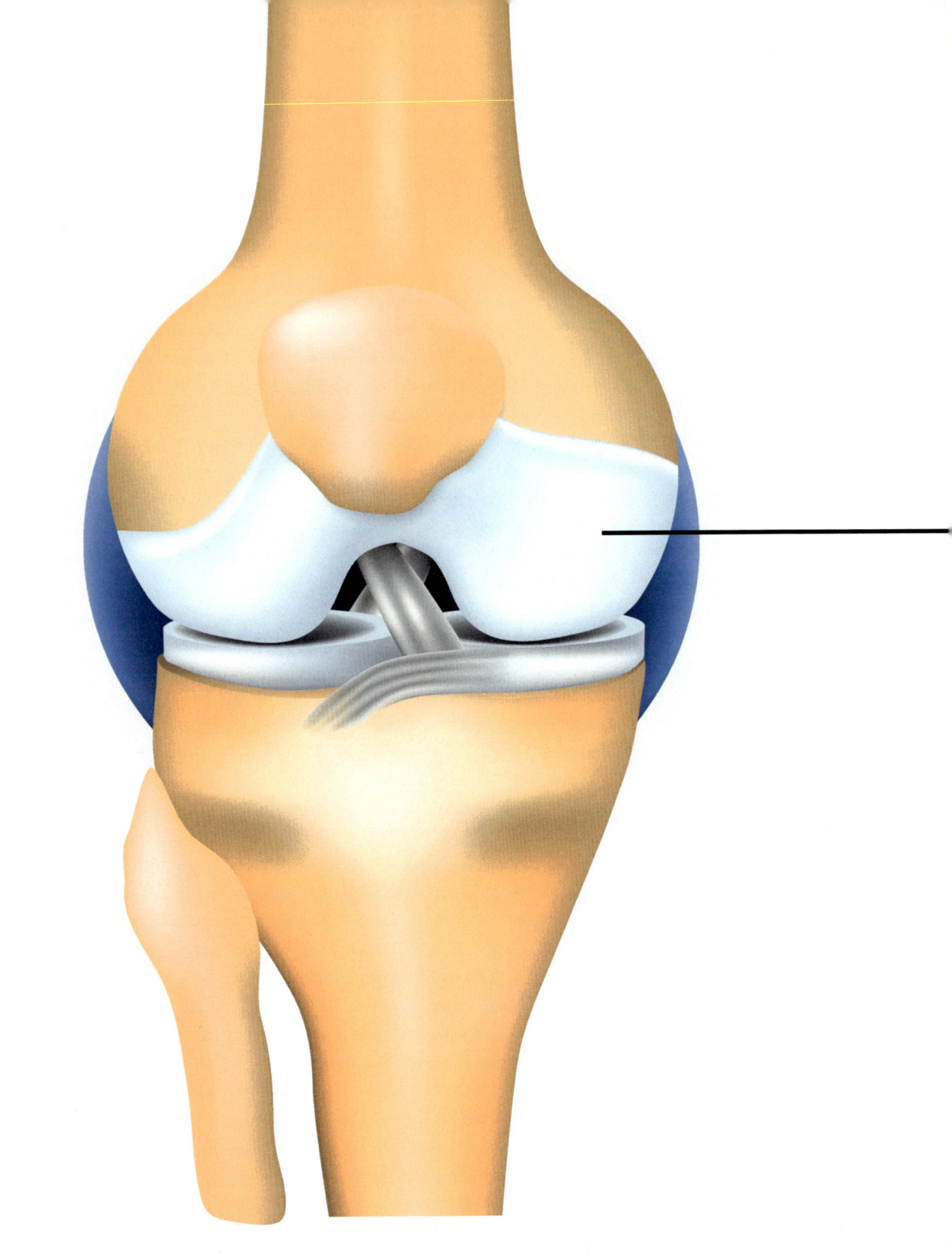

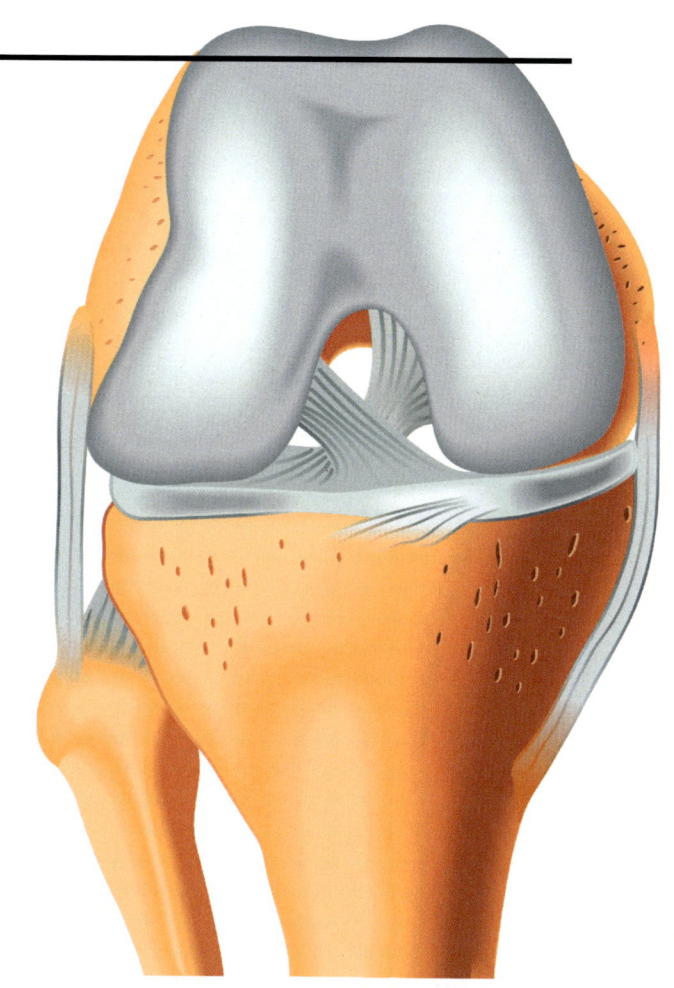

cartilage

Some of our baby bones are made of cartilage. As we grow bigger and heavier, the cartilage is slowly replaced by harder bone and some smaller bones combines to form a single bigger bone. Cartilage is a flexible material found between your bones.

The skull is the home for your three-pound brain. The brain is protected by a number of bones.

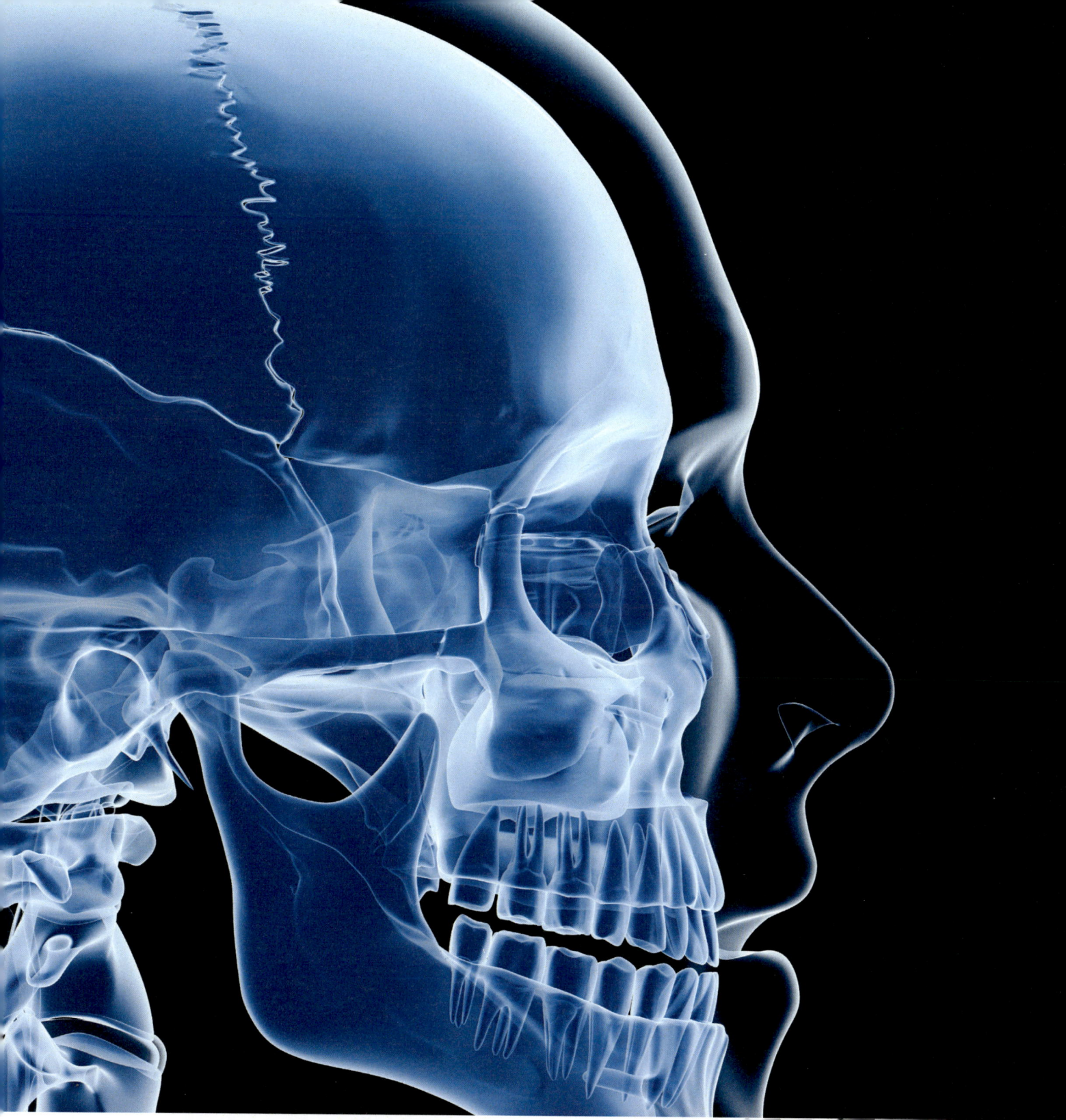

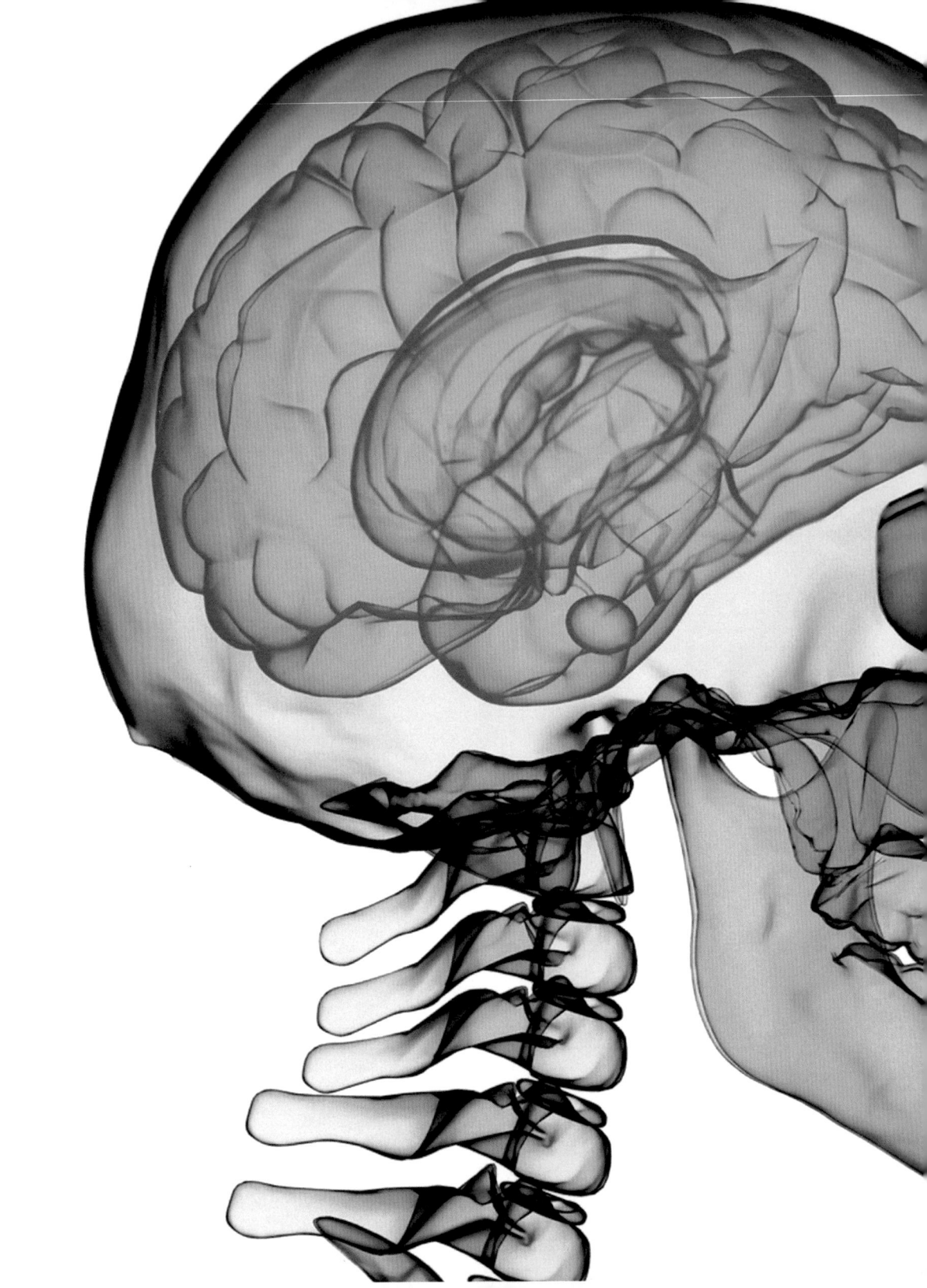

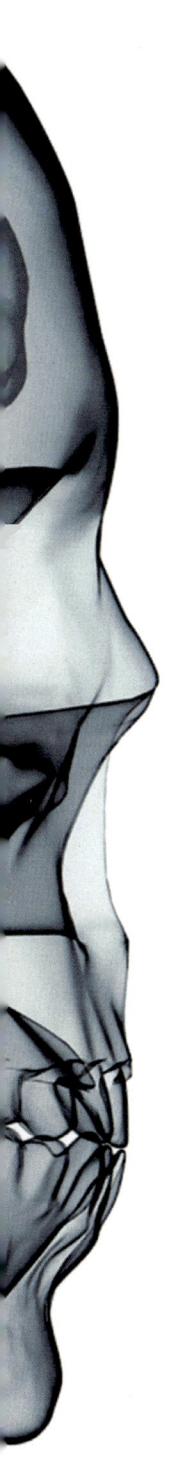

Your skull is the most complex part of the skeleton. Your skull is like a natural helmet that protects the brain. It also helps shape your face.

A newborn baby has soft spot on top of its head called the fontanelle. It helps the skull be flexible as the baby's brain grows very quickly. As the person gets older, the bones of the skull join together and close the soft spot.

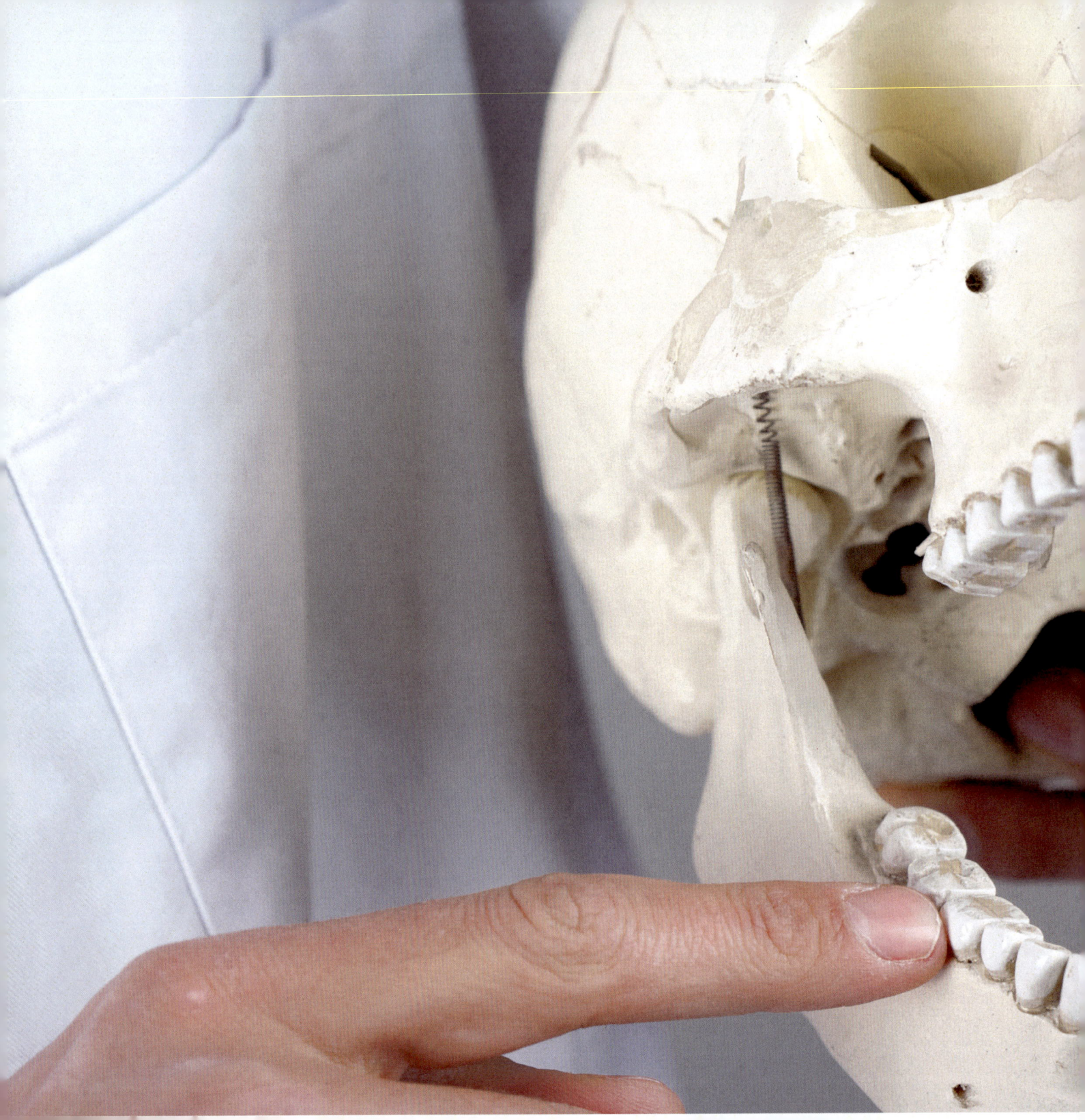

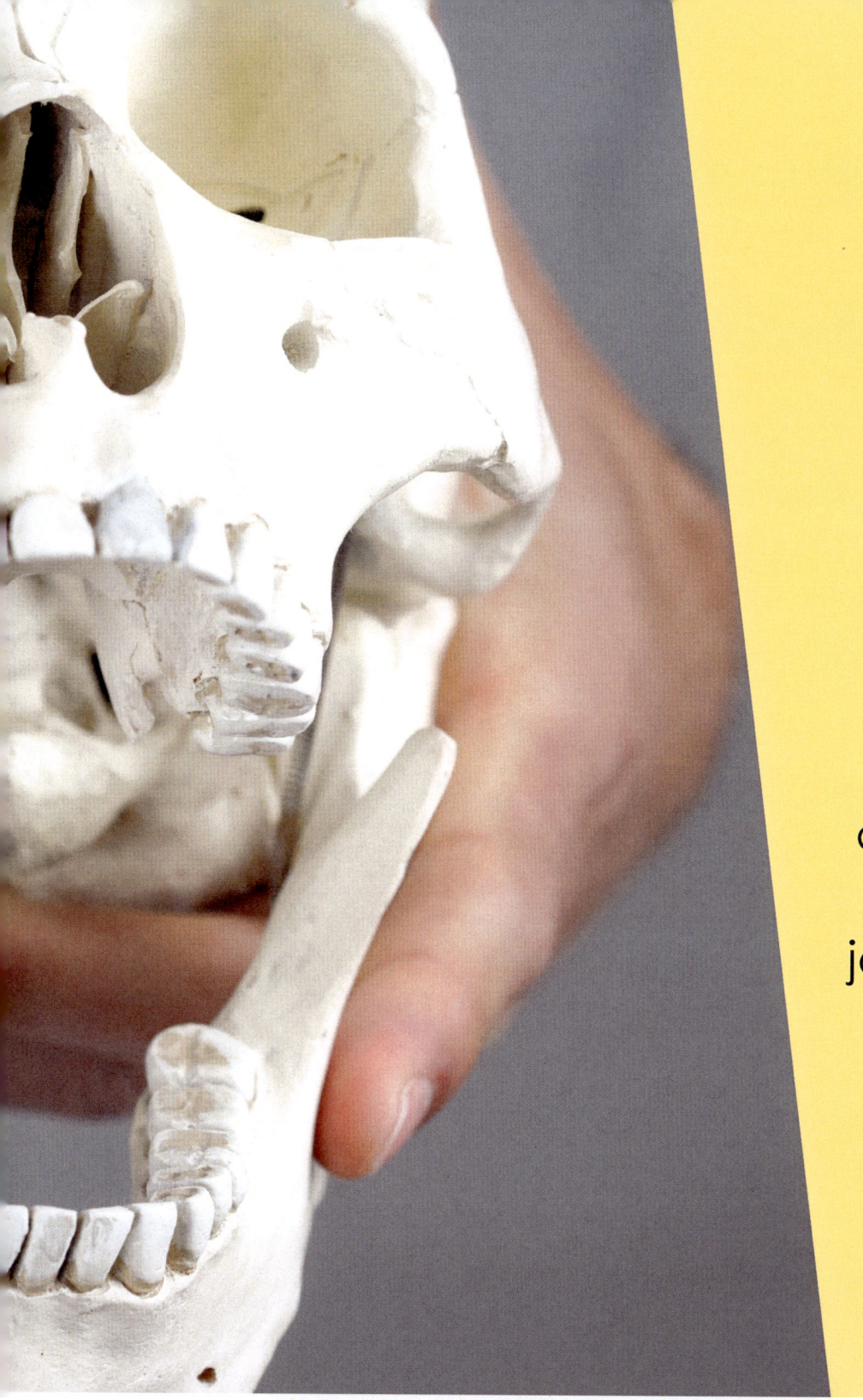

The bone from your chin to where it hinges just under your ear is the jawbone. The jawbone is the only bone in your skull that can move. Your movable lower jaw helps you to breathe, speak and eat.

The spine is a part of the skeleton that easy to check and recognize. It is at the center of your back and you can feel its bumps under your fingers. The spine lets you twist and bend and helps hold you upright.

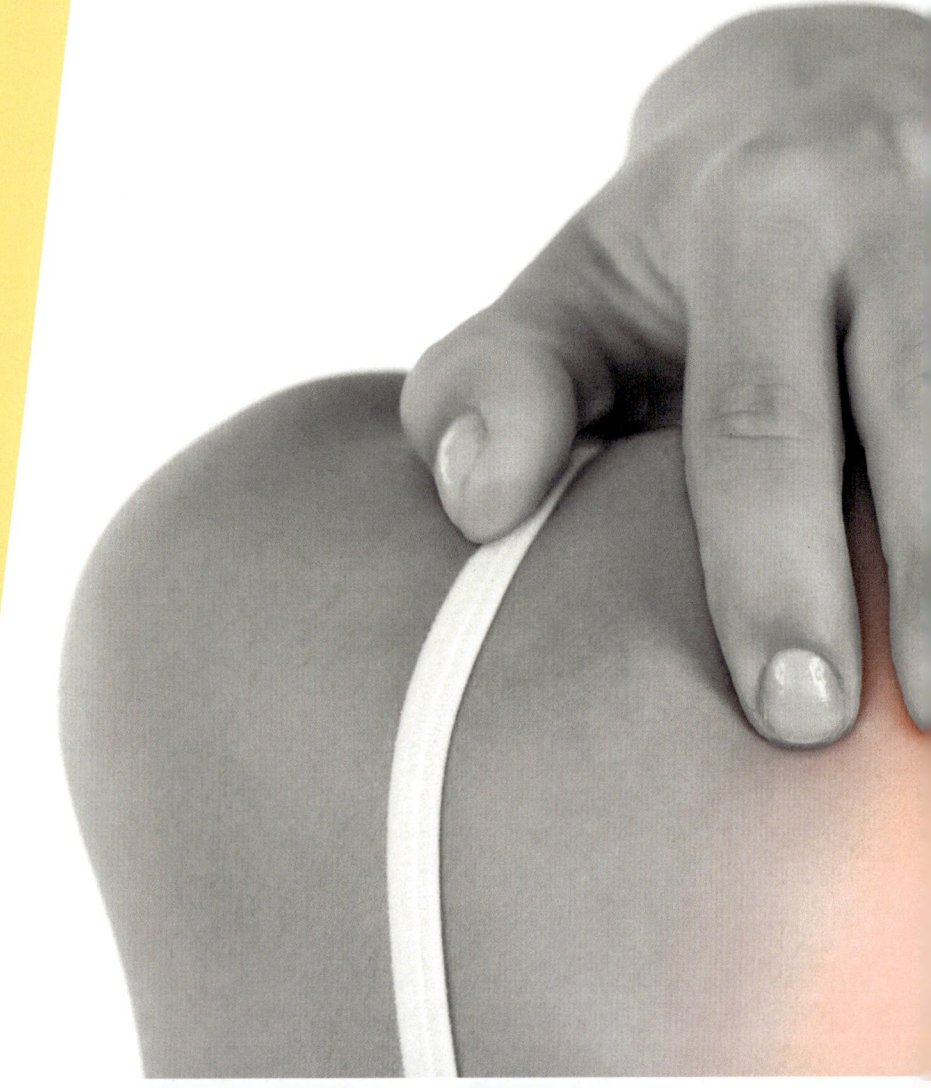

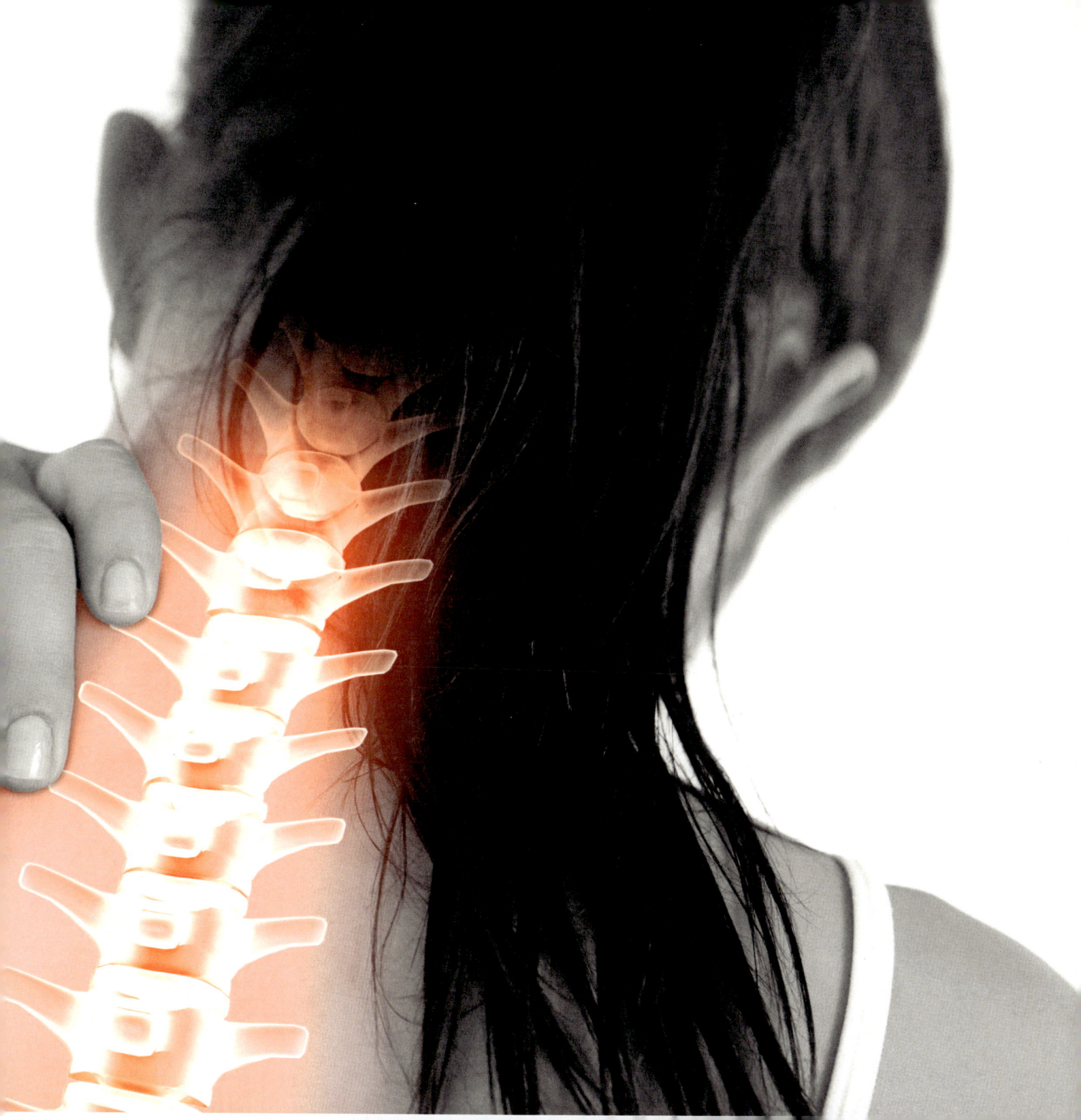

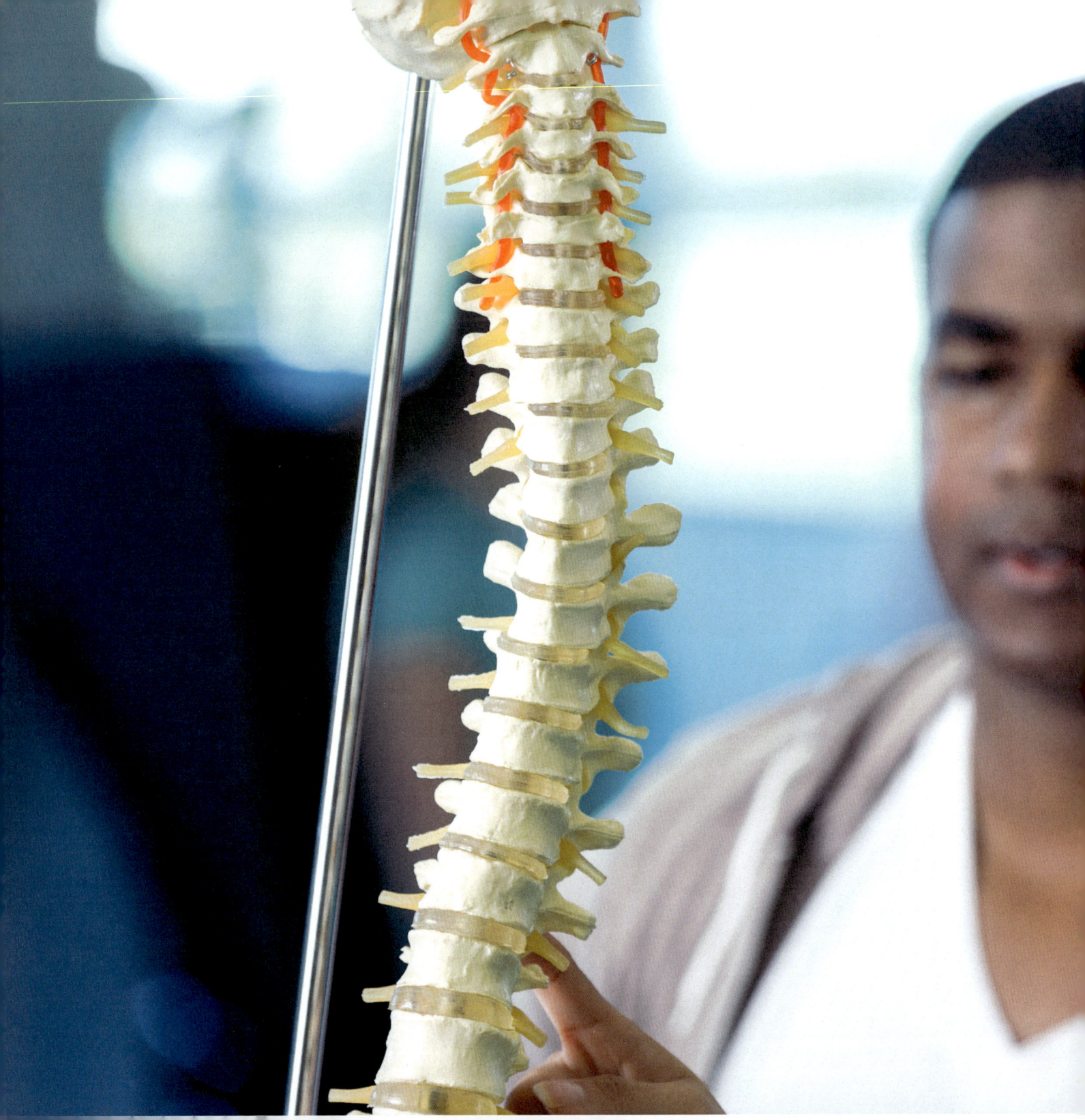

The spine protects the spinal cord, which works as a pathway for messages between brain and rest of the body. It has connecting nerves to all parts of your body, so your brain knows what is happening and can give instructions.

The spine is a column of bones running down at the back of your body. Your spine has 26 bones which are like loops with wings on the sides and back. These bones are called vertebrae.

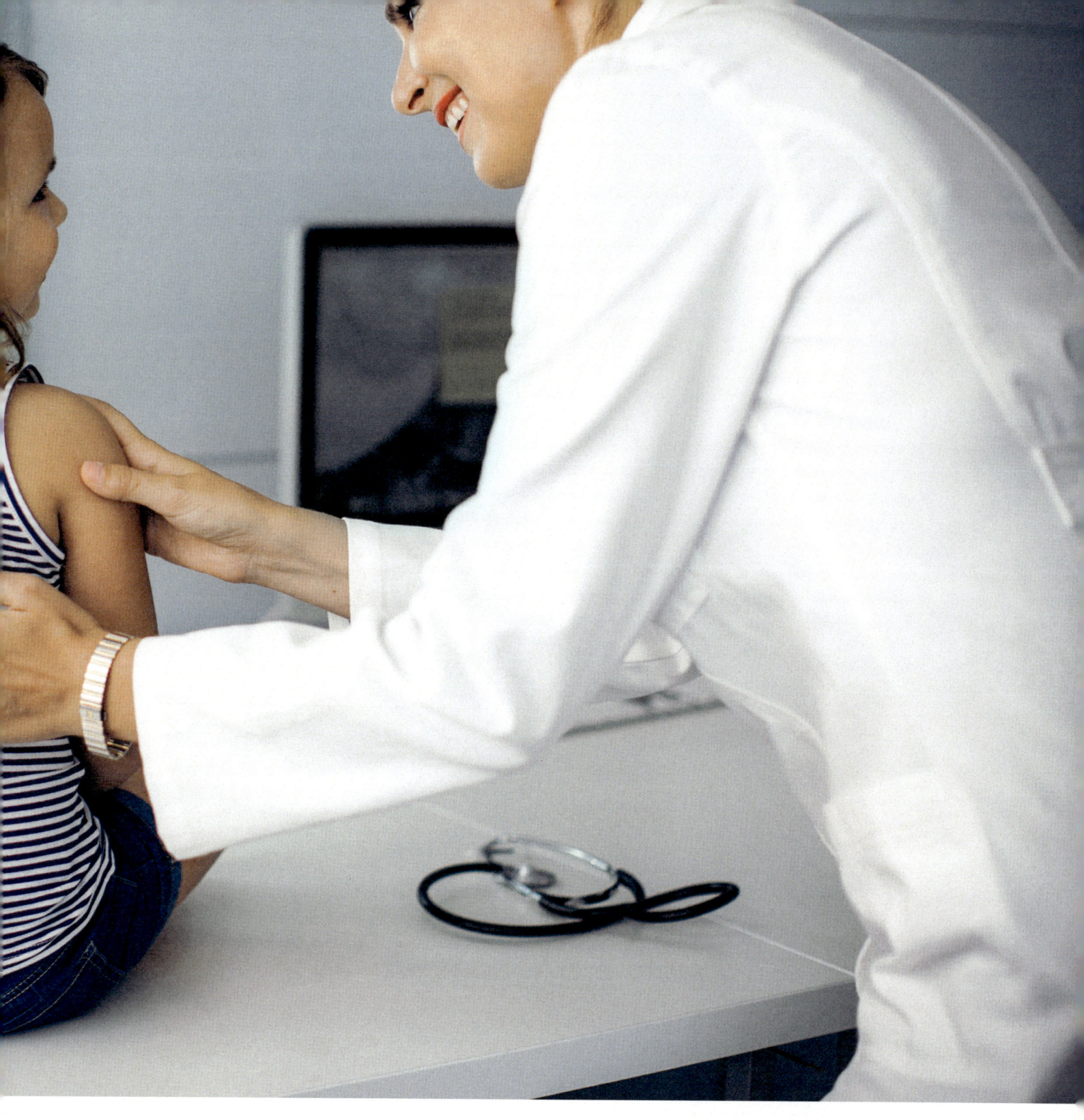

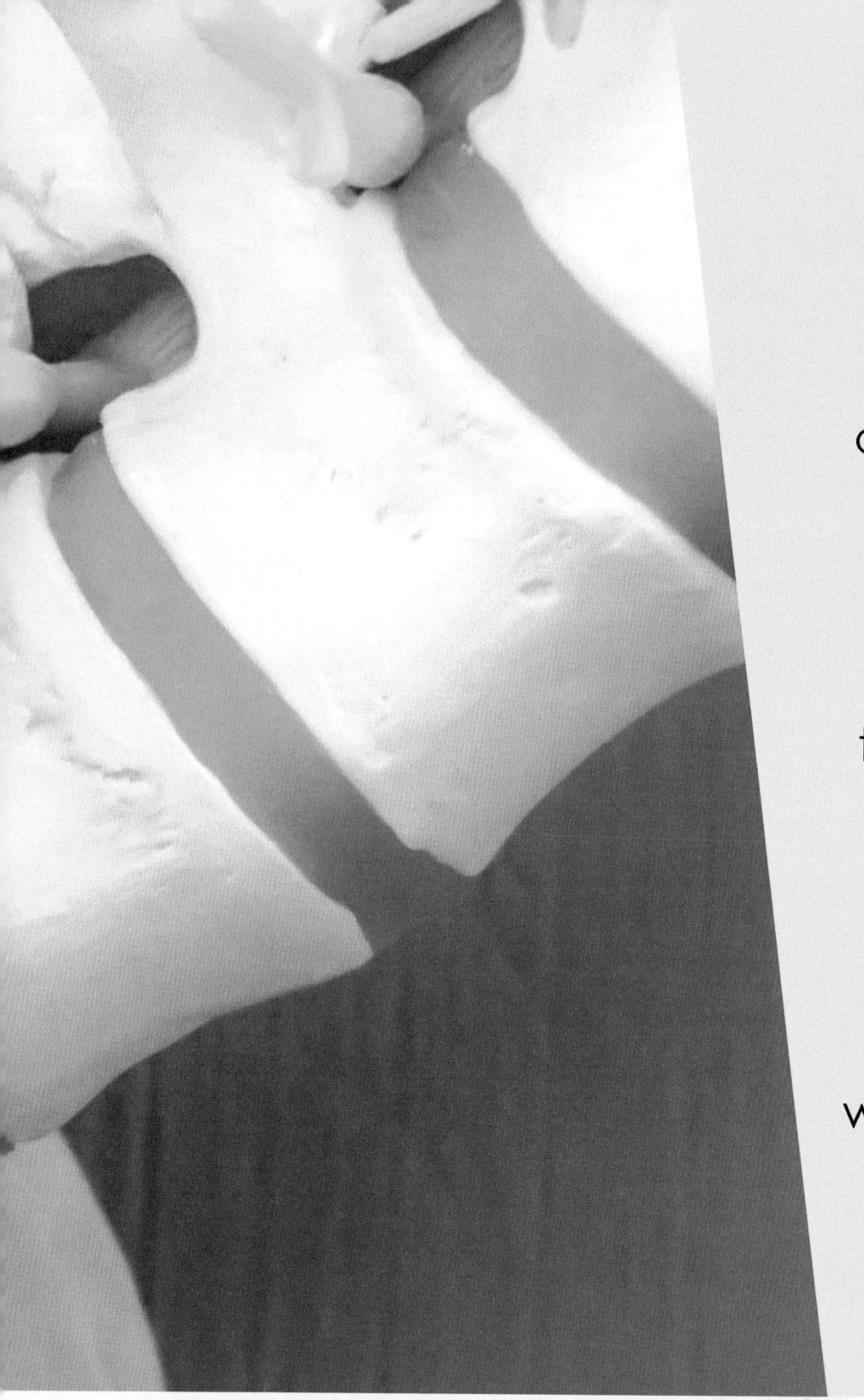

Between the vertebrae (ver-tu-bray) are small discs made of cartilage, so the bones do not rub on each other. Each vertebra has a tough and thick section that supports your weight. There is also a hole in each vertebra where the spinal cord passes through.

The ribs are the protective cage around your lungs, liver and heart. The ribs are curved bones. Your can feel your ribs under the skin of your chest.

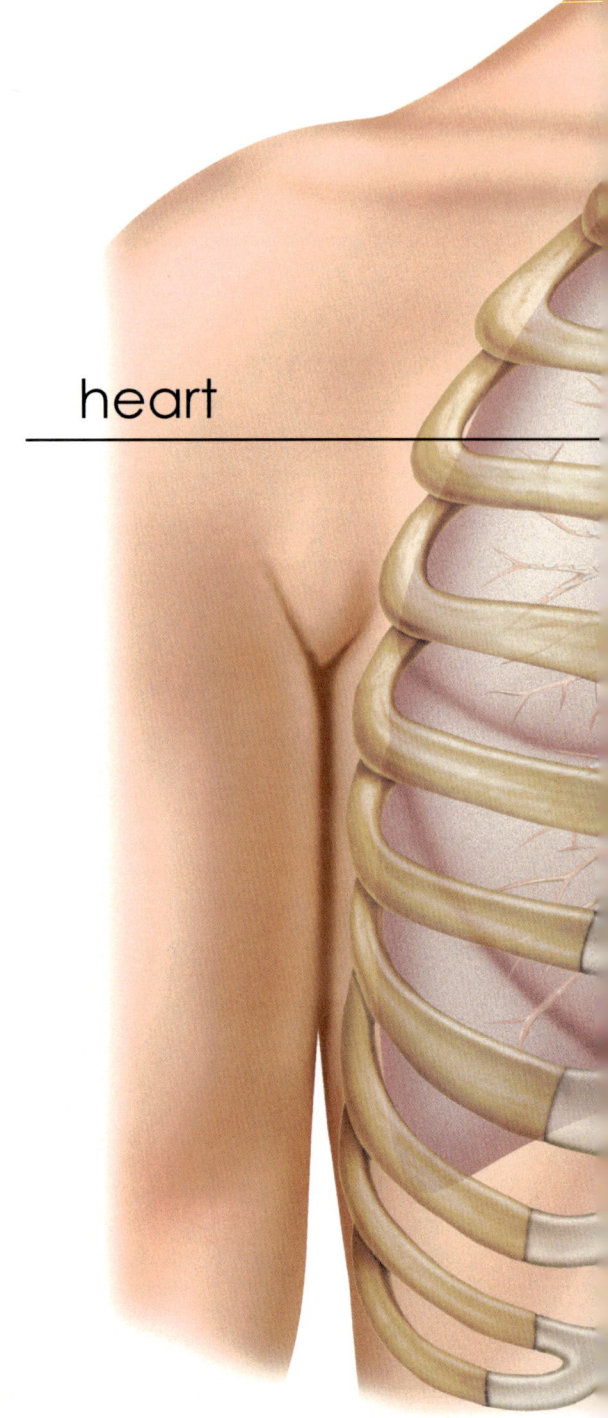

heart

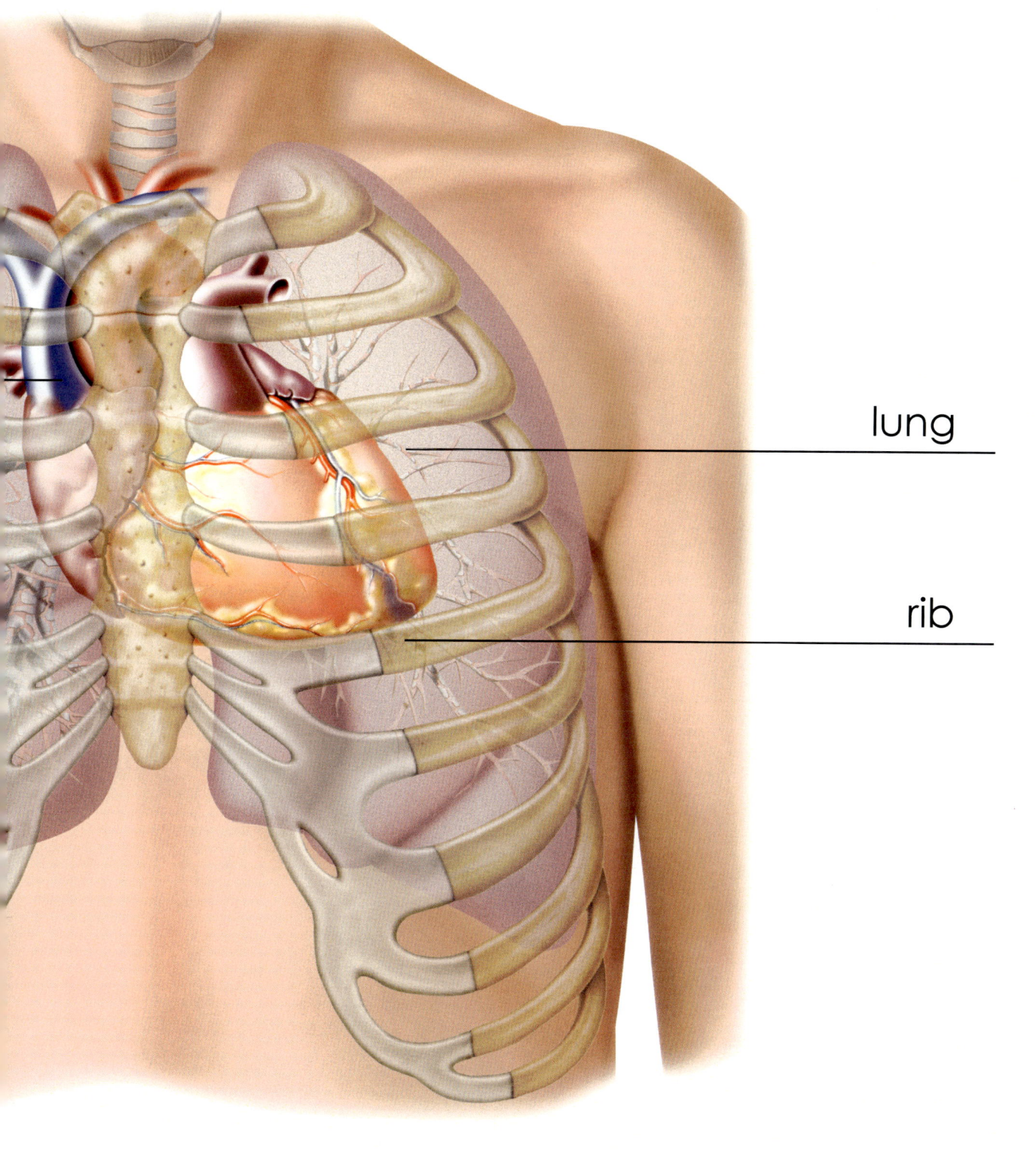

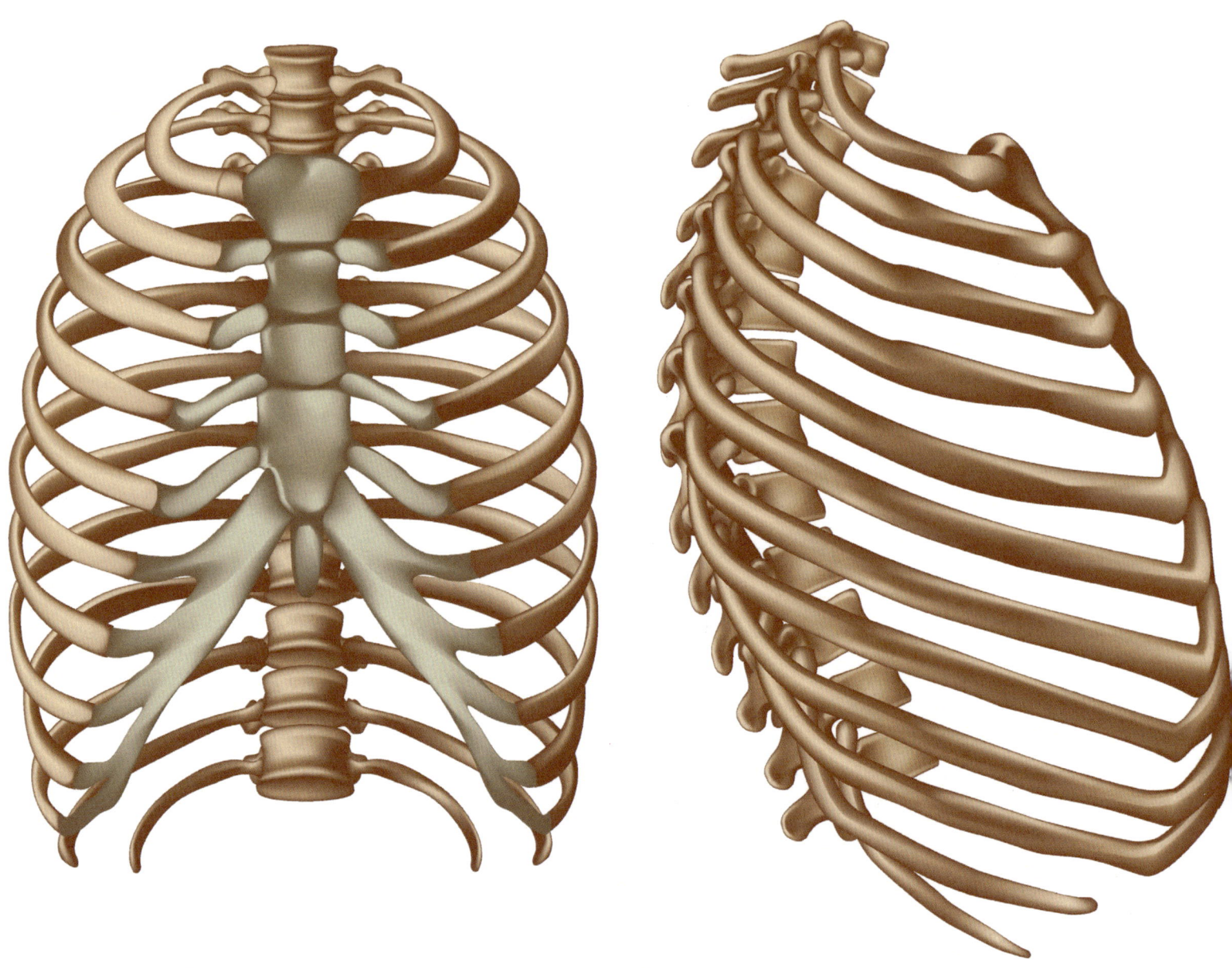

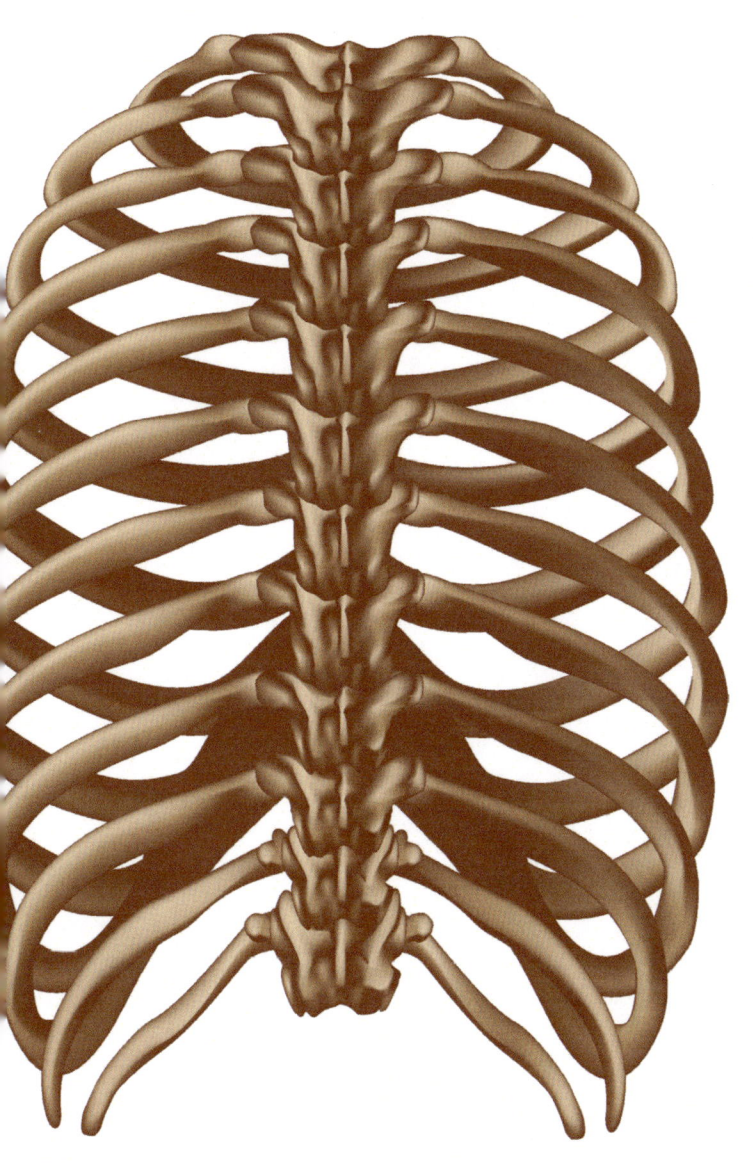

Ribs come in pairs; the left and right side are mostly identical. There are usually 12 pairs of ribs in the human body. Each rib is attached to the ribs above and below it by muscles and ligaments.

Every time you breath, your rib cage enlarges by 3 to 5 cm. it is actually quite delicate. It can be damaged by sports activity, accidents or even when you sneeze.

Do broken bones heal? Bones can re-grow and repair on their own. If you need to keep still, a doctor might assist and give you a cast to wear until the bone had repaired itself. When a bone breaks it is called a fracture.

Here are fun facts about bones. The thigh bones are the biggest bones in your body. The smallest bone is found in the ear. The area of our body with the most bones is the hand, fingers and wrist where, there are 54 bones.

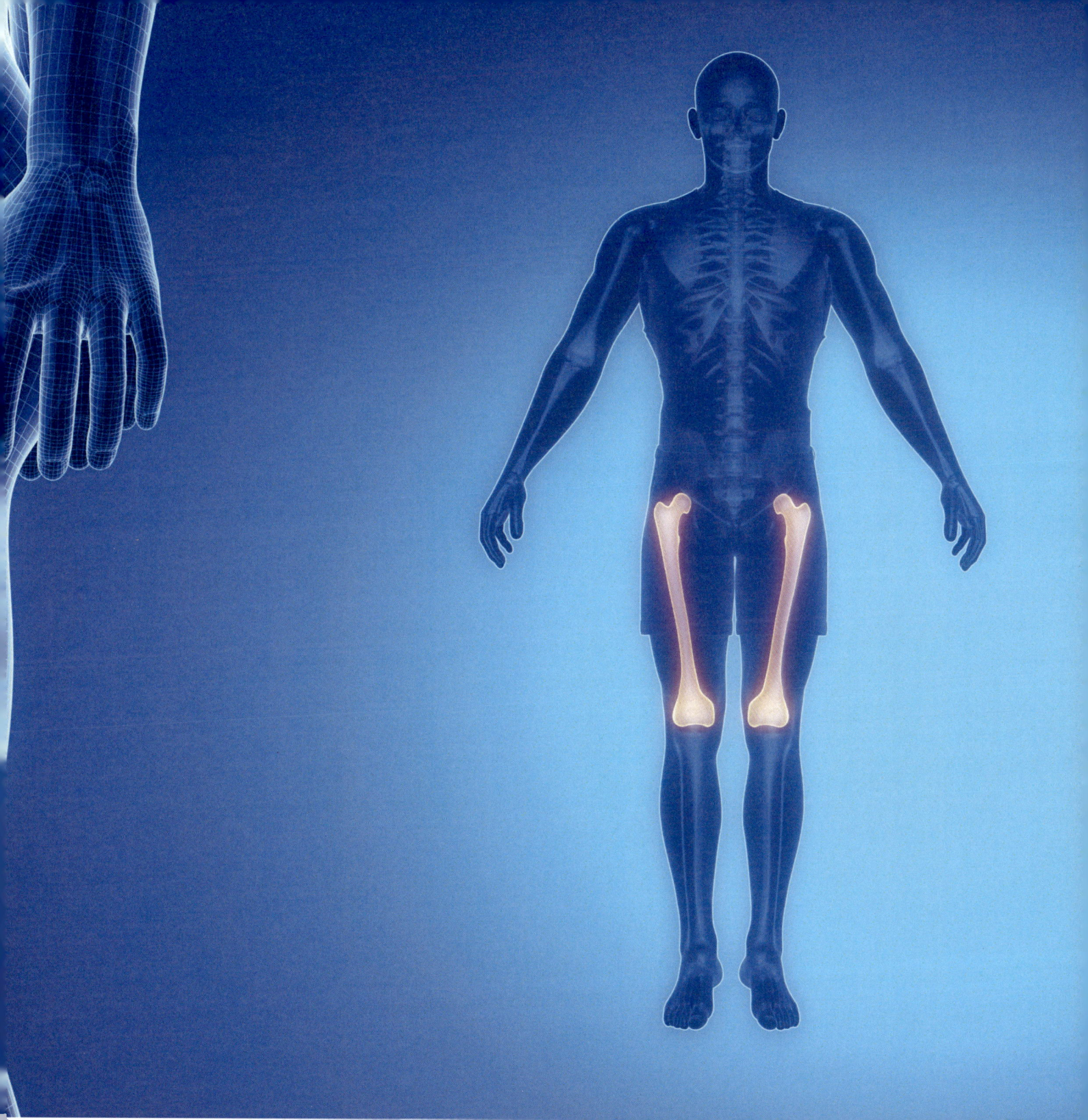

Your bones help you every day, so make sure you take care of them, too. You only get one body. Eating healthy foods with plenty of calcium, getting plenty of exercise and looking after your back are ways to take care of your bones.

Made in the USA
San Bernardino, CA
17 April 2018